St. Molaissi's, Kilmacnessan

First published 2005 AD
© Wooden Books Ltd 2005

Published by Wooden Books Ltd.
12a High Street, Glastonbury, Somerset

British Library Cataloguing in Publication Data
McDonnell, H.
Irish Round Towers

A CIP catalogue record for this towering
tome is available from the British Library

ISBN 1 904263 31 3

Printed and bound in Great Britain
by The Cromwell Press, Trowbridge

IRISH ROUND TOWERS

St. Kevin's, Glendalough

by

Hector McDonnell

with illustrations from ancient sources
and by the author

To Anthea,
who gave me that dratted book on Irish round towers twenty years ago, and with many thanks to Nelson Bell, for allowing us to use many images from his collection of books.

Pictures have been taken from "Early Christian Architecture in Ireland" by Margaret Stokes, London, 1878, "The Towers and Temples of Ancient Ireland" by Marcus Keane, Dublin, 1867, "Notices on the Round Towers of Ulster" by G. M. Hills, Dublin, 1854 and "The Ecclesiatical Architecture of Ireland" by George Petrie, Dublin, 1845.

Further Reading: M. Stokes, The Early Christian Architecture of Ireland, Dublin 1979; H. McDonnell, Margaret Stokes and the Irish Round Tower, Ulster Journal of Archaeology, 1994; R. Stalley, Irish Round Towers, Dublin 2000.

Drumbo

Glendalough

IRELAND.

The names of places at or near
which the views have been taken
are underlined thus ___ Killarney.

Scale of English Miles

INTRODUCTION

The round towers of Ireland are by far the largest relics of the ancient Irish church. Some are over thirty metres tall. They were always built as part of monastic sites, and while some still dominate the landscape around the greatest ancient Irish monasteries, others now stand completely alone, as all other traces of the monasteries that built them have vanished. They are as pure an expression of geometry as architecture can offer, their slim stone and mortar cylindrical bodies topped with conical stone cap roofs. Usually they are freestanding, though a few are incorporated into churches, in particular at two of the most important of all Irish monastic sites, Glendalough and Clonmacnoise. Interestingly, the Irish for a round tower is a *clog teach*, a bell house, and the plural is *clog tigh*.

These towers are extremely enigmatic. The Irish built on a modest architectural scale, and its churches are normally very small indeed. Why then should so many monasteries have built such impressively tall towers? This book will try to give some answers to these puzzles, and even pose a few more questions.

Glenarm, Co. Antrim

NEAR EASTERN CONNECTIONS
and Holy Land influences

Missionaries from Britain and Gaul Christianised Ireland in the fifth and sixth centuries, but the story of the round towers will lead us to the Near East, so it is as well to know how longingly the early Irish Church looked eastwards beyond Rome to the Holy Land.

Irish high crosses were inspired by pilgrims' descriptions of the Jewelled Cross erected on the orders of St Helena at the site of the Crucifiction, while their central circles first appear in Coptic Egypt. Even more remarkably the only accurate plans we have of the Holy Land's early churches were made on Iona, from the accounts of Arculph, a Gaulish pilgrim, who was shipwrecked there on his way home, while several important features of early Irish illumination, such as crosses embedded in fields of interlace, seem to derive from Syrian Christian sources.

Equally astonishingly Rahan, an early Irish church, has Armenian-looking architectural features, possibly because a nearby monastery housed Armenian monks. They had come as fugitives from Islam, as did others whom Charlemagne employed as architects. Indeed the only high crosses comparable to those of the British Isles are found in Armenia and Georgia. They were probably also inspired by St. Helena's Jewelled Cross.

High Cross of Durrow   *High Cross of Muredach*

ABBOTS AND CROSSES
the very first Irish towers

The towers must at least predate their first mention in the annals, the burning of Slane's clog teach in AD 950. We also know the identity of two tower builders. Cormac Ui Cillin, who died in 964, was the "comarb of Tuaim-greine", and built built both its church and clog teach, and Colman Conailleach, abbot of Clonmacnoise, 904-921, was called the "joy of every tower." This suggests that he built several. Colman was a busy man, as he also sculpted the Cross of the Scriptures at Clonmacnoise according to the historian Françoise Henry. "In Irish monasteries", she said, "as in Benedictine ones, manual occupations alternated constantly with spiritual exercises, and manual work often took the form of art or craftsmanship."

These two architect-builders were abbots, the leaders of their spiritual communities, and clearly they would only have erected their towers for a serious religious purpose.

Clonmacnoise

MILLS, MORTAR & MONASTERIES
Ireland acquires some Roman technologies

Irish monasteries were genuine centres of knowledge and inventiveness. In the sixth century they encouraged an agricultural revolution, with Roman-style tools, mills, cattle and crops. A century later, one of them, Nendrum, built the earliest known tidal mill in the world. These advances went hand in hand with the production of spectacular artworks, like the Book of Kells, the Ardagh chalice and the High Crosses, the largest sculptured monuments of ninth century Europe.

It is therefore not so surprising that the monasteries threw themselves so enthusiastically into something so novel as tower building in the tenth century. The use of mortar had just reached Ireland, so the towers appear during a general architectural revolution and the building of the country's first big churches, such as the cathedral at Clonmacnoise.

Today these towers often stand in obscure places, but a thousand years ago these were prestige sites, places like the tiny hamlet of Armoy, in county Antrim, which was then the royal seat of the kingdom of Dalriada, or deserted Monasterboice, one of the chief monasteries of Leinster. Several other towers must have had similar remarkable origins, though now they stand forlorn, the reasons for their existence lost beyond recall.

Drumeskin

Antrim

Devenish

Roscrea

Abernethy

Kells

BUILDING IN THE ROUND
no need for corner stones

Like the towers, virtually all other Irish buildings of the time had circular plans. The Irish lived in round wattle and daub houses, and round palisaded forts called raths. Only the churches were rectangular, in deference, presumably, to Roman tradition. The earliest were tiny, but after mortar reached Ireland in the eighth century larger churches started to appear. Only these, and the round towers themselves, were built with mortar.

Hoists, pulleys, and scaffolding were devised to raise stones and mortar to higher and higher levels, and the holes for scaffolding beams are still visible in some tower walls. A further problem was that the types of available stone varied enormously. Some areas had plentiful sandstone, which could be neatly carved and shaped, but in other places there was only iron-hard basalt or granite, though even here the larger stones were hammered into a curve.

Drumlane

GEOMETRY

an octave in the round

The approximate height of twenty-six towers is known. Three are exceptionally short, and one unusually tall, but the rest average out at nearly 100 Roman feet, while all the base circumferences average approximately 51 Roman feet. Seemingly the builders wanted perfectly proportioned towers, 100 feet high and 50 feet round.

The four top windows are usually oriented towards the cardinal points of the compass, and the towers also taper, by varying amounts. At Ratoo the diameter shrinks by a quarter, most are considerably less, and at some the taper is minimal.

The towers were divided into several wooden floors, resting either on corbels or ledges. and lit by small windows. Access was presumably by ladders or steep steps through openings in the floors.

Another surprise: their elegant stone and mortar conical caps were not part of the original concept, for the annals describe several towers losing their roofs in storms. These were probably slate and wood constructions, but after a few disasters the builders devised the solid vaulted caps we now see.

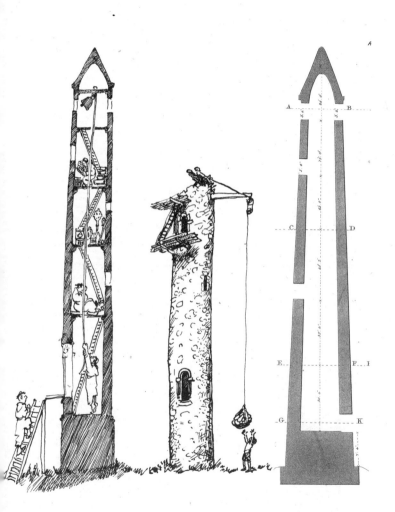

DOORS AND WINDOWS
up in the air

Nearly all the towers have entrances well above ground level. This is usually explained as being so the defenders of the monastery could pull up their ladders during an attack. However some have ground level doorways, and others are so high that ladders tall enough to reach them would not fit inside.

A few doorways are carved, but the towers are striking for their simplicity, contrasting starkly with the monasteries' ornate high crosses. The windows are also simple, some square, some round-headed, some triangular, marking the changes from the angularity of early Irish forms to the curves of true arches.

The later towers did in fact break away from simple forms and in indulge in Romanesque ornamentation, usually to the doors, but once to the cornice (*Devenish*), and once to a window (*see Timahoe below*).

Kells

Timahoe

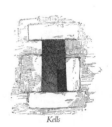

Kells

Cashel

Dysert Aengus

Dysert Aengus

Antrim

Lusk

Dysert Aengus

Kilmacduagh

Swords

Lusk

Clonmacnoise

Lusk

Roscom

SITING

looking at the way in

The towers' positioning also followed a pattern. They usually stand near the western end of the monastery's most important church, with their doors pointing at the church entrance. This inspired one historian to propose an explanation:

Groups of pilgrims would visit a monastery, see its holy sites, adore its religious images, and attend its rituals. The tower's bells would ring out for the more significant moments, and then, from its high doorway, the monks would display the community's holiest possessions to the crowd as they emerged from the church. Such monkish theatrics were a normal and deliberate ingredient of church ritual. The annals reveal that ancient bells, crosiers, relics and manuscripts were certainly stored in the towers in times of danger.

Of course, each tower has a different story to tell, but here are four examples to give some idea of them ...

Kilbannon

Iniscelltra

CASHEL
of the bishop-kings

In the late fourth century the Eóghanachta dynasty established their royal fortress on this rock. They possibly came from Wales, where Irish colonies were being forced out under Welsh pressure, but in consequence they had contact with the Roman world and therefore called their fortress a *castellum* (Cashel). Until the 10th century this dynasty were the over-kings of Munster. Tradition says that St Patrick came here and baptized the reigning king, and at least four kings were also bishops or abbots. Brian Boru made himself king of Cashel in about 978, and his descendant gave Cashel to the archbishop of Munster in 1101. The astonishing Romanesque cathedral, built by Cormac MacCarthy, King of Desmond, was superceded by the great Gothic cathedral beside it in the 13th century.

The tower is probably 11th century, though the Eóghannachta king-bishop Cormac MacCuilleannain (died 908) has been suggested as its builder. It is the earliest surviving structure on Cashel, and as its doorway looks towards Cormac's north porch an earlier church may well have stood here. The round-arched doorway has seven irregular voussoirs, with a plain raised moulding running round the door. The tower is built from well cut and dressed local sandstone blocks, with square headed windows for the lower floors and triangular-headed ones on the top floor, which are approximately oriented to the cardinal points.

CLONES
an early tower

Clones monastery was founded by St. Tigernach, who had previously been the bishop of Clogher, and died here in 549. It became an important centre, the principal abbey of the local kingdom, of Uriel. A fine 10th century High Cross survives, as do fragments of a Romanesque church at some considerable distance from the tower, and a fine 12th century monolithic gabled house-tomb containing the bones of St. Tigernach. "All the churches" of Clones were destroyed in a raid in 836, which was a year of terrible Viking raids, warfare and destruction throughout the country. Devenish was also destroyed by them that year. Clones was burned again in 1096, but there is little other information about the site.

The tower is complete up to bell-floor level, but its cap is missing, and the straightforwardly unembellished form of its construction suggests an early date, probably 10th century. Its masonry consists of roughly coursed and dressed sandstone, and there is only a slight batter. The doorway is a simple rectangle, narrow, with approximately straight jambs and a monolithic lintel. It faces east, but there are no traces of any church nearby. All the windows are equally plain and square-headed, and are capped by flat lintels.

DEVENISH
Ulster's finest

St. Molaise founded Devenish in the 6th century, and Vikings destroyed it in 836. Its remains include a 12th century tomb-shrine, a 13th century church, and a late medieval high cross. The tower is of finely cut sandstone, the door has a true arch and architrave, with a large angle-headed window above it. The unique carved cornice at the top has a band of lozenges, scrolls and four human heads, possibly representing the evangelists or Irish saints. An earlier tower was destroyed in 1157 when the king of Fermanagh 'was burnt in the cloicteach by his own kinsmen.' Its foundations are nearby.

The new king of Tara was 'treacherously' killed in Kells cloicteach in 1076, during inauguration rituals, and kings are associated with other towers, so they had royal as well as monastic significance. Perhaps their elevated doors had the same symbolism as Charlemagne's throne, sited on the upper floor of Aachen cathedral so that everyone else was below him. An abbot could also have emphasised authority in this way.

The Devenish tower has as elaborate carvings as any Irish church. Perhaps there was also a chapel inside it, as there was in the towers on the St. Gallen plan (*see page 36*).

ARDMORE
a noble survivor

The monastery is said to be a fifth century foundation of the pre-Patrician missionary St. Declan. Nearby are his tomb, his well and the stone which transported his bell and vestments over from Wales.

The tower is probably 12th century, as are the remarkable biblical scenes carved on the ruined cathedral. It is made of evenly coursed sandstone blocks with three prominent string courses and a cornice. It has the most pronounced batter of any Irish tower and inside are some elaborately carved corbels.

In 1642 an English army beseiged Irish troops in Ardmore castle, and about 40 more in the tower, armed with two muskets. All were hanged after surrendering. In the 1860s the capstone was shot off but was replaced. Under the tower's foundations were skeletons oriented towards the east, indicating that it was built on top of a Christian graveyard.

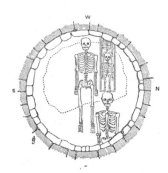

ANCIENT DESTRUCTION
and persistent pillaging

Some towers vanished so long ago that we only know of them through references in ancient annals:

"AD 950 The clog teach of Slane was burned by the foreigners (the Vikings of Dublin), with its full of relics and distinguished persons, together with Caeineachair, Lector of Slane, and the crosier of the patron saint, and a bell, the best of bells."

Annals of the Four Masters

"1121 A great wind-storm happened in December of this year, which knocked the conical cap off the clog teach of Armagh and caused great destruction of woods throughout Ireland."

Annals of the Four Masters

"1126 A great hosting by Connor MacFergall O'Loughlinn, together with the people of the North of Ireland, went to Meath. They burnt Trim, both clog teach and church, and these full of people."

Annals of Ulster

Armagh's tower of 1121 was the second one built there. It finally vanished in the Cromwellian period. Lightning had destroyed the first one in the 990s.

Rathmichael

Drumcliffe

Killashee

Mungret

Ardmore

Aghavuller

SURVIVAL
and some more destruction

Today some seventy-three round towers still exist, while several more have disappeared relatively recently. The Protestant bishop of Raphoe knocked his down in the 1630s, to make room for his palace, and Killeshin's was demolished "in three days' work" in 1703. In the early 1800s two local landowners were restoring a ruined church at Downpatrick (*below left*) as the Anglican cathedral but disagreed violently about its round tower, which stood beside St. Patrick's supposed grave. Unfortunately the one who admired the tower was called away on business, whereupon the other demolished it, and used the stones for rebuilding the church.

Other towers disappeared less dramatically. The fallen drum at Maghera was carted off as building material, while a tower that appears in early views of Dublin, the 'Old Tower of Michael le Pole' (*below right*), succumbed to the town's expansion. By the nineteenth century a red brick schoolhouse stood on the spot, which has now given way to the level tarmac of a car park.

SPECULATIONS
and absurdities

Irish antiquarians often plunged into some very peculiar round tower speculations. Here are some examples:

The towers were for ancient Irish anchorites, but, unlike St Simon Stylites in Syria these Irish hermits needed roofs, because of the constant rain.

Danes built the towers (they had built all England's prehistoric monuments too) and all that was sophisticated of early Irish culture, from interlace to filigree (this avoided attributing any ingenuity to the native Irish).

The towers were phalluses. Two nineteenth century young men, William O'Brien and Marcus Keane, got very excited. The towers had to be lingams, remnants of an enormous Hindi-Irish civilization, the Cuthite Empire, which had covered all Eurasia and America at the time of Nebuchadnessar. There are therefore Cuthite round towers in India, Ireland, ancient Mexico and Peru (*opposite*).

Similarly exotic speculations continue: were the towers monkish lookouts against approaching Vikings? Or semaphore stations, communicating from one end of Ireland to the other? Or the central spikes of sundials? Or the amplifiers of enormous bells? Or huge energisers of the Earth-Grid?

East India

East India

Persia

Peru

Central America

PRESTIGE
of abbots and warriors

The truth seems to be reasonably simple. Tall was beautiful even then. Like modern skyscrapers these towers demonstrated the power and wealth of their owners. As for their being a defence against the Vikings, many were built in areas the Vikings controlled, and most attacks were made by other Irishmen. The towers were built in what were very troubled times, and as Ireland then had no stone castles, they were very impressive-looking strongholds at the time.

Though the towers obviously had a defensive role, they were not particularly effective (*see the gazeteer for grizzly details*). Bolt-holes at several doorways show that people expected to lock themselves inside and having the doors at a height was an obvious help. Hardly a year went by without one petty kingdom waging war against another one and the monasteries, as repositories of much treasure, were obvious targets.

In fact many European Romanesque keeps had elevated entrances, and at Lake Chiemsee there is an early ninth century keep whose entrance is a full storey above ground level. So this defensive device was in use before the first Irish towers

Tory Island

31

A WOMAN WITH AN ANSWER
but several more questions

In the 1870s a remarkable woman, Miss Margaret Stokes, pointed out that there were some very ancient round bell towers, or *campanili*, beside the Byzantine basilicas of Ravenna. But why should the Irish have copied them? Miss Stokes looked desperately for an explanation. Perhaps there were once similar bell towers in northern Europe, which wandering Irish monks could have seen them more easily. But then why had they all disappeared?

Miss Stokes found one round medieval tower in Brittany, and then noticed that many large Romanesque churches had round towers attached to their western facades. They were centuries later than the earliest Irish ones, and housed staircases, but externally they looked so similar that she could not believe there was no connection. But what? Where were the earlier ones in Europe, apart from the examples in Ravenna, and why should the Irish have even known about these? Had the rest of Europe trekked to Ireland and then copied its towers? That was just too implausible. It was equally implausible that Irishmen built Europe's big Romanesque churches, as they failed to build anything on that scale at home.

RAVENNA
the city of the round campanili

Ravenna is famous, not for its round campanili but for its spectacular Byzantine churches and their mosaics. It flourished as the western capital of the Byzantine empire until it was captured in the 750s and given to the papacy, after which its churches were handed over to monastic communities

Probably in the late eighth century the first European bell tower was built beside the church dedicated to San Apollinare, Ravenna's patron saint, at Classe, the city's enormous port, once the great harbour of Roman and Byzantine fleets. However Classe was dying, as it was silting up (Venice would soon arise to take its place), and in 858 the local archbishop moved San Apollinare's remains to another Byzantine church in Ravenna itself. Here he built a crypt under the church identical to the one at Classe to house the saint's bones, and also another round campanile beside it (campanili were later heightened).

Soon the idea caught on, and monasteries all over Ravenna were putting up round campanili beside their Byzantine churches. Not only that, but there were also two Irish monastic communities in Ravenna at the time, so the idea was passed back to Ireland, and before long they were building their own round bell towers too, paying no attention when the fashion changed and the Italians started building the square ones with which we are so familiar.

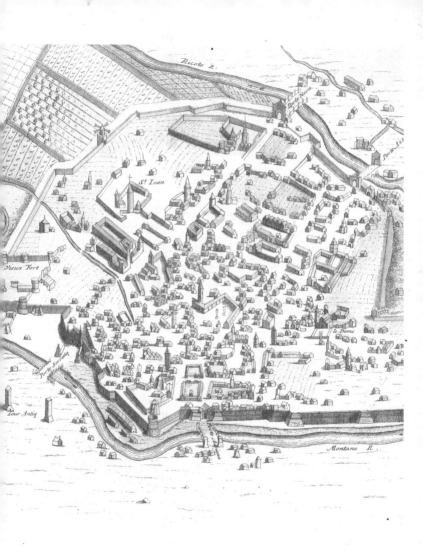

Ricote R:

Porta Nova

Porte Ass.

St Iean

Vieux Fort

Porte Serviae

le Dome

Tour Antiq

Montane R.

35

CHARLEMAGNE
Charlemagne and the round tower

The Irish were not alone in being inspired by Ravenna. Charlemagne visited it in the 780s, demolished several Byzantine buildings, and transported their parts to Aachen to build himself a 'Roman' palace there, with an imperial chapel imitating the greatest Ravennan church, San Vitale.

The idea of round campanili impressed him too, for round bell towers were built at two of his great ecclesiastical buildings. St Riquier, in northern France, (circa 790) had four round towers, while Fulda (790-819), has a circular foundation by its entrance for another one. Humbler churches like St Johannisberg (circa 800-900) followed, which had a single circular belfry at its western end.

Even more remarkably, a plan was drawn up in about 810 for a new monastery at Sankt Gallen, with two freestanding round towers set at an angle to the church entrance, echoing the Irish geometrical relationship between church and tower.

Charlemagne had forced all monasteries inside his empire to follow the same Benedictine disciplines, but as Ireland, the papal states and Ravenna were outside his control, they continued with the old system, with each monastery drawing up its own rules. The Irish must therefore have felt that their monastic system had the papal seal of approval, and that the round campanile, which broadcast its own community's religious hours, was an important architectural statement of this reality.

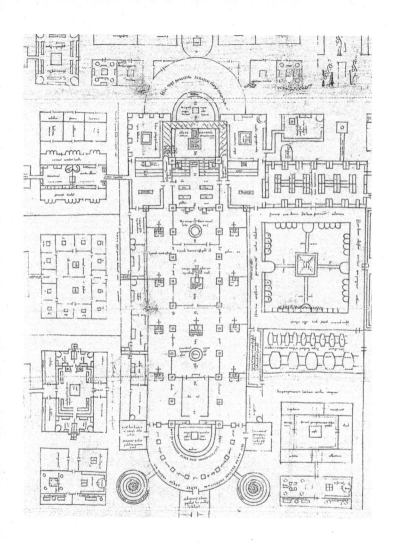

Northern European Round Towers
and Charlemagne's church builders

Round bell towers were therefore being built in Europe about a hundred years before the first Irish clog teach, and continued to be popular long afterwards in other peripheral areas such as Denmark, north Germany and Poland. In East Anglia the round belfry attached to the west end of a simple rectangular church as had happened at St. Johannisberg was particularly popular, possibly because its last king, St. Edmund, had close connections with Charlemagne's court and brought over a large German retinue, including, perhaps, some church builders. There are 220 East Anglian churches with round belfries standing today. This idea spread northwards too, as far as the Orkneys.

Nor should we forget Charlemagne's cathedral of St. Riquier. Its round corner towers inspired the standard embellishment of the larger Romanesque churches which Margaret Stokes had noted. There is hardly a Romanesque cathedral north of the Alps which does not have round towers at its corners.

Magnus   *Deerness*

St Maurice, Epinal

St Genevieve

Genrode, Hartz

MINARETS AND LIGHTHOUSES
looking out to see

Tradition maintains that the first of Ravenna's round bell towers, at San Apollinare in Classe, is built on the foundations of a Roman lighthouse. The campanile would certainly have been useful, fulfilling some functions of ancient lighthouses, as a look-out post and an indicator of the harbour for incoming ships, moreover Caorle, further north on the Adriatic, also has a round campanile by its harbour which doubled as a sighting position for ships until a taller square campanile was built closer to the sea. Several other campanili also have the tradition that they stand on the foundations of Roman lighthouses. But why?

The explanation seems to hinge on Egypt. When the Moslem conquerors took Alexandria they followed an Islamic precept that places of prayer should be those of the most significant activities of the community, and therefore established a mosque and a round tower beside the beacon of the Pharos, the enormous lighthouse which was one of the Seven Wonders of the World, only slightly shorter than the Great Pyramid, and the tallest building in the world until the Woolworth Tower, New York's first great skyscraper, was built.

As the Moslems moved along the southern Mediterranean coast they built forts called ribats at the ports, and on each ribat was a tall round tower, a minaret. Just like the Pharos they were also sighting positions for ships, and got their name because the word minaret meant a lighthouse.

41

COUNTING THE HOURS
and cross fertilisations

There were direct contacts between the Islamic ports of North Africa and Ravenna, so the idea of the new lighthouse-cum-religious-hour-proclaimer reached the Ravennans easily. The only important change they made was replacing the muezzin's call with bells to broadcast the religious hours. Nevertheless both religions established the same thing – the imposition of particular hours on their communities. It was the beginning of modern time keeping.

The Greco-Roman world divided time into twelve hours between sunrise and sunset, and another twelve hours of night. Which was fine, except that the length of daylight varies, so the hours lengthened and shortened with the seasons. Their first public clock was the Tower of the Winds in Athens inside which a hydraulically operated statue pointed at a revolving pillar inscribed with lines indicating the hours' varying length.

Islam and Christianity inherited these altering hours. The Arabs were particularly impressed by a clock in Gaza with twelve doors through which a statue of Hercules emerged at the appropriate hour of the day. Lights appeared behind each door at night. They built a similar clock for their first great mosque, at Damascus, which required many workmen to keep it going. The caliph Harun Al Rashid sent Charlemagne one, and another was installed at Ravenna, but there were apparently none in Ireland!

CLOCKING IN
keeping a watch on time

The Irish round towers were designed, like the minarets and the campanili, to broadcast these religious hours. That is why the word *clock* originally meant a bell, as in *clog teach*. St. Benedict stipulated that the day's work should first stop for a meal at the ninth hour, which was when Christ had died. However this was intolerable for any workforce, as noon, the ninth hour, was in the middle of what we now call the afternoon. Noon then discreetely slipped backwards to midday, so the workforce could have their lunch, although noon was now the sixth, not the ninth hour. Noon, in other words, was an early victim of a labour dispute.

Many simple methods were tried to count the hours properly. Sundials helped, as did marked candles at night time. King Alfred burnt six every night so as to keep up with his devotions, and also had clepsydrae, which poured water from one basin into another. Indeed this search for accuracy ultimately caused the invention of clockwork, which was the death knell of the old, variable hours. In Ireland all these systems were tried, and their annals' observations of astronomical events frequently note the hour, and a night watch, showing that someone in each monastery kept a careful eye on the time. Indeed, that is why today we call a timepiece a watch.

BELL CASTING
a monkish mystery

Early Christian bells looked like cowbells and were rung by hand, but the round towers used heavier, cast bells. Irish custom even defined a bell ringer's status: "Noble his work when the bell is a clog teach's, humble when it is a hand bell."

Bell casting was developed in the eighth century, and the process was a jealously guarded monastic secret, so the towers were also by-products of a new technology. Surviving Irish cast bells are not more than a foot high, but Margaret Stokes rang a small dinner bell from a clog teach's windows – and it was heard half a mile away, so even they could be effective.

Ravenna's bell towers still function, but soldiers melted down Clonmacnoise's bells in 1552 for cannons, and presumably any other round tower bells too. An old Irish law ordered ships to provide ropes for a local clog teach, so bells were probably rung much as today, hung high in the towers and pulled from below. A few clog tigh, such as Dromiskin and Balla, have been reused as bell towers in recent times, so their ancient purpose has not entirely disappeared.

Ancient Bells of Ireland

Bell of St Patrick

Clog Beannaighthe

47

THE LEANING TOWER

a swan song

In an important sense the Irish clog tigh continued the lighthouse function of their Italian and Islamic predecessors. They were good viewing positions for monks watching for whoever might be approaching, and landmarks for anyone trying to find them. The monasteries were pilgrimage centres, so many would be looking for these towers, through what was then a largely untamed landscape, a rolling green sea of natural woodlands. Indeed all church towers continued to have this use for a long time. That, in fact, is the origin of the steeplechase: a cross–country horse race, from one church tower to the next.

And so to the last and most famous round bell tower. In the 12th century Pisa was the greatest naval power of Italy. They drove the Muslims out of southern Italy, and built Pisa's ecclesiastical complex, reviving the spirit of earlier times. It has a cathedral, an enormous baptistery, and of course the round campanile which leans so dramatically. It was sited beside the cathedral, and not far from the city's quays. It therefore could, symbolically at least, continue the dual purpose of San Apollinare in Classe, or Caorle, or indeed the Pharos of Alexandria. Ironically, the last Irish round towers were being built at much the same time.

In the Leaning Tower's uppermost arches the old bells still hang, but no one would dare ring them now.

Cashel

COMPLETE GAZETEER

Aghadoe; Ruinous. 3 km NW of Killarney on R562, Co. Kerry. 5.5m high, 4.6m diam. Monastery founded by St. Finnian the Leper in 7th C. A ruined 12th C. church stands beside it. [94]

Aghagower; Ruinous half-tower. 5 km SE of Westport, Co. Mayo, on N59. 15.9m high, 5.0m base diam. Monastery founded by St. Senach in 7th C. Beside it is a ruined 12th-15th C. church. [23]

Aghaviller; Half-tower. 2 km E. of Killmaganny, Co. Kilkenny. 9.6m high, 4.9m base diam. Medieval church and tower-house in the graveyard, and foundations of 12th C. church. [80]

Annaghdown; Vanished. monastery by Lough Corrib, 19 km N of Galway, founded by St Brendan of Clonfert, whi died there 577. His sister, St Brigid, had a nunnery nearby. The tower was built in 1238, the latest known. [26]

Antrim; Complete tower with original conical cap. Close to Antrim town, Co. Antrim, S. of the A6. 28m high, 4.8m base diam. Its monastery first mentioned in 7th C., but all ruins removed c.1800. Cross over door. [8]

Ardbraccan; Vanished. 5 km W of Navan. Known through a reference in the annals stating that it fell in 1181. [49]

Ardfert; Vanished. Collapsed in 1771. 8 km NW of Tralee, Co. Kerry. Monastery founded by St. Brendan the Navigator in 6th C. [95]

Ardmore; Complete with cap. Beside village, Co. Waterford, on R673. 29.2m high, 5.0m diam. Monastery founded by St. Declan, a pre-Patrician saint, in 5th C. An 11th C. cathedral stands beside. Fine sculptures on tower and church. 40 Irish soldiers beseiged in it by the English in 1642, later hanged. [89]

Ardpatrick; Ruined stump. 8 km S of Kilmallock, on R512, Co. Limerick. 3m high, 5.3m diam. Monastery reputed founded by St. Patrick. Described in 1826 as a "fine round tower which fell a few years since". [87]

Ardrahan; Low stump. 12 km N. of Gort, Co. Galway, on N18. 2.9m high, 4.7m diam. Little known. [35]

Armagh; Vanished. Beside cathedral, Co. Armagh. Struck by lightning 1888, "burnt with its bells" 1020, lost its cap 1121. [14]

Armoy; Fragmentary tower. 2 km E. of Armoy village, Co. Antrim, on A44. 10.8m high, 4.6m base diam. Its monastery founded by St. Olcan, disciple of St. Patrick, at royal centre of Dalriada. [6]

Balla; Truncated tower. 12 km SE of Castlebar, Co. Mayo, on N50. Monastery founded by St. Mochua in 637 or 694, destoyed by fire 1197. Until c.1800 it stood to about 15m and was then reduced in 1830s for use as a bell tower. [22]

Boyle; Damaged tower built into wall of 12th C. abbey as a corner turret. In town of Boyle, Co. Roscommon. 3.6m high, 5.1m base diam. Little known, tower still standing in 1603. [39]

Brigown; Vanished. Collapsed after a storm in 1720. In 1807 the remnants were used to build a house. Near Mitchelstown, Co. Cork. [88]

Cashel; Complete, with cap. On rock, beside Cashel town, Co. Tipperary. 27.9m high, 5.3m base diam. Ancient royal site. In 1101 the entire rock was given to the Church by Murtagh O'Brien. Gothic cathedral built in 13th C. stands, roofless, beside the tower. [84]

Castledermot; Complete, castellation replacing conical cap. 12 km N. of Carlow, Co. Kildare, on N9. 20.1m high, 4.7m base diam. Monastery established by St. Dermot c.600. Important centre of 9th C. Culdees. Plundered by Vikings 841 and 867. Two fine High Crosses in the churchyard and a Viking's graveslab. [68]

Clondalkin; Complete, with original cap. In centre of village, 8 km SW of Dublin, Co. Dublin. 27.5m high, 4.0m base diam. Monastery founded by St. Cronan in 7th C., plundered by Danes in 832 and Olaf the White, the founder of Dublin, built a fort here in 852. [59]

Clones; Complete tower, missing cap. In town centre, Co. Monaghan. 23m high, 4.5m base diam. Monastery founded by St. Tighernach, died 549. In the graveyard is his 12th C. stone gabled house-tomb. A High Cross stands nearby. [16]

Clonmacnoise; Two towers, (a) complete with missing cap, (b) complete with cap and attached to church. On E. bank of Shannon river, 11.5 km S of Athlone, Co. Offaly, on R444. (a) 19.3m high, 5.6m base diam. (b) 16.8m high, 3.8m base diam. Monastery founded by St. Kieran, died 548. Tower (a) constructed by Fergal O' Rourke, king of Connacht, died 964, its cap struck off by lightning 1145. Tower (b) known as Temple Finghin. The bells of the towers were taken away by English soldiers in 1552 for canons. Fine monastic site with several ruined churches and High Crosses. [62]

Cloyne; Complete, battlements replacing conical cap. In the town of Cloyne, Co. Cork. 30.5m high, 5.2m base diam. Monastery founded by St. Colman, died 604. [90]

Connor; Vanished. Stump removed in 19th C. from Connor graveyard, Co. Antrim. [7]

Cork; Vanished. The tower fell in 1738, and was described as being over 100ft high. It stood beside St. Finbar's cathedral. [91]

Derry; Vanished after 1689. Co. Londonderry. The

1.Tory Island; 2. Raphoe; 3. Derry; 4. Tamlaght; 5. Dungiven; 6. Armoy; 7. Connor; 8. Antrim; 9. Rams Island; 10. Nendrum; 11. Drumbo; 12. Downpatrick; 13. Maghera; 14. Armagh; 15. Killeevy; 16. Clones; 17. Devenish; 18. Drumcliff; 19. Killala; 20. Turlough; 21. Meelick; 22. Balla; 23. Aghagower; 24. Kilbennan; 25. Kilcoona; 26. Annaghdown; 27. Roscam; 28. Killeany; 29. Rath Blamic; 30. Dysert O'Dea; 31. Drumcliff; 32. Tuaimgrainey; 33. Killinaboy; 34. Kilmacduagh; 35. Ardrahan; 36. Roscommon; 37. Oran; 38. Kilbarry; 39. Boyle; 40. Tomregon; 41. Drumlane; 42. Inishkeen; 43. Louth; 44. Faughart; 45. Dromiskin; 46. Monasterboice; 47. Kells; 48. Slane; 49. Ardbraccan; 50. Donaghmore; 51. Lusk; 52. Trim; 53. Tullaghard; 54. Duleek; 55. Swords; 56. Kilmacnessan; 57. St Michael le Pole; 58. Taghadoe; 59. Clondalkin; 60. Killashee; 61. Oughterard; 62. Clonmacnoise; 63. Seir Kieran; 64. Kildare; 65. Rathmichael; 66. Kilcullen; 67. Glendalough; 68. Castledermot; 69. Timahoe; 70. Roscrea; 71. Inis Cealtra; 72. Killeshin; 73. Kellistown; 74. Ferns; 75. Fertagh; 76. Kilkenny; 77. Tullaherin; 78. St Mullins; 79. Kilree; 80. Aghaviller; 81. Liathmore; 82. Limerick; 83. Emly; 84. Cashel; 85. Dysert Oenghusa; 86. Kilmallock; 87. Ardpatrick; 88. Brigown; 89. Ardmore; 90. Cloyne; 91. Cork; 92. Kinneigh; 93. Rosscarbery; 94. Aghadoe; 95. Ardfert; 96. Rattoo; 97. Scattery.

53

monastery was founded by St. Columba in 546. Local tradition said it had a silver bell of miraculous power. [3]

Devenish; Complete, with cap. On Devenish Island, Lough Erne, Co. Fermanagh. 25m high, 4.8m base diam. The foundations of an earlier round tower are beside it. The monastery was founded by St. Molaise, died 563. Site destroyed by Vikings 836 and again 1157. Beautifully carved cornice. [17]

Donaghmore; Complete tower with damaged cap. 5 km NE of Navan, Co. Meath, on N51. 26.6m high, 5.0m base diam. Monastery said to have been founded by St. Cassanus, a disciple of St. Patrick. The 15th C. church ruin incorporates a fragment of an earlier church. Crucifiction carving above doorway and two heads. [50]

Downpatrick; Vanished. Co. Down. Demolished c.1800 so as to repair the cathedral with its stones. [12]

Dromiskin; Unusually low tower with cap. 10 km SW of Dundalk, Co. Louth, on the N1. 15.2m high, 5.2m base diam. Monastery reputedly founded by St. Patrick, and repeatedly plundered between 948 and 1043. [45]

Drumbo; Lower third still stands. 5 km NE of Lisburn, Co. Down. 5.4m high, 4.9m base diam. Monastery said to date from St. Patrick's time. [11]

Drumcliff; Lower third of tower. 6.5 km NW of Sligo, Co. Sligo, on N16. 9m high, 5.0m base diam. Monastery founded by St. Columba in 575 and frequently plundered. Tower was struck by lightning in 1396. A fine High Cross stands in the graveyard. [18]

Drumcliff; Ruined stump. On N85, 4 km NW of Ennis, Co. Clare. 11m high, 4.9m base diam. Monastery founded by St. Conald. [31]

Drumlane; Nearly complete tower. 1 km S. of Milltown village on R201, Co. Cavan. 11.6m high, 5.1m base diam. Monastery founded by St. Maedoc in 6th C. Two indistinct carvings (birds?) on N. face. [41]

Duleek; Ghost of small round tower impressed into side of 15th C. church belfry. 4 km SW of Drogheda, Co. Meath, on R150. 14m high, 5.2m base diam. Trad. site of first stone church in Ireland, built by St. Cianan, died 489. Brian Boru's body was laid here after Battle of Clontarf 1014. Tower struck by thunderbolt 1147. [54]

Dungiven; Vanished. Co. Londonderry. The Augustinian priory had an attached round tower at the SW corner c.15m high. Undermined by treasure-seekers and fell in 1784. [5]

Dysert Oenghusa; Nearly complete tower missing upper windows. 3 km W. of Croom, Co. Limerick, on the N20. 20.7m high, 5.3m base diam. Monastery founded by Oenghus the Culdee, died 815. Ruin of medieval church stands beside it. Fine carving round doorway. [85]

Dysert O'Dea; Ruined. On R476, 5 km S. of Corrofin, Co. Clare. 14.6m high, 5.9m base diam. An important early

monastic site with 12th C. High Cross, founded 7th or 8th C. by St. Tola. [30]

Emly; Vanished. 12 km W. of Tipperary. The cathedral and tower were completely burnt in 1058 by Turlough O'Brien. The monastery was founded by St. Ailbhe in the early 6th C. [83]

Faughart; Bare featureless stump. 2 km N of Dundalk, off the N11, Co. Louth. 5.8m diam. Traditional birth-place of St. Brigid. Monastery founded by St. Monenna in 6th C. Edward the Bruce was killed here in 1318. [44]

Ferns; Incomplete tower on square base. 12 km NE of Enniscorthy, Co. Wexford, on N11. 18.2m high, 2.9m diam. An engaged tower, part of 12th C. church, both dating from the foundation of an Augustinian priory here by Dermot MacMurrough in 1160. [74]

Fertagh; Complete, missing cap. 4 km N. of Johnstown, Co. Kilkenny, on N1. Monastery founded by St. Kieran in 5th C. Devastated 1156 by Murtagh MacNiale, high king of Ireland, who burnt the round tower with the lector inside it. Doorway removed by a farmer in 1830s for his kitchen fireplace. [75]

Glendalough; Three round towers, *(a)* complete tower with cap, 30.5m high, 4.5m base diam; *(b)* engaged complete tower with cap on St. Kevin's church, 14.1m high, 2.0m base diam; and *(c)* vanished engaged tower on Trinity church, 15m high, 4m base diam. 4 km W. of Laragh, Co. Wicklow, on R755. Monastery founded by St. Kevin, died 618, and became an important centre of learning. Raided and destroyed many times between 8th and 12th C.'s. Tower *(c)* collapsed in a storm in 1818. [67]

Inis Cealtra; Complete tower missing cap.' 1 km offshore from Mount Shannon, Co. Clare. 22.3m high, 4.6m base diam. Ruins of 4 churches on the island, and Two High Crosses. Settlement established by St. Columb of Terryglass in 7th C. Twice burnt by Vikings; later under patronage of Brian Boru. [71]

Inishkeen; Delapidated lower part of tower. Village 5 km N. of R178, Co. Monaghan. 12.6m high, 4.5m base diam. Founded by St. Dega in 6th C. Partly demolished in 19th C. for use as a belfry. [42]

Kellistown; Destroyed 1807. Village lies 8 km SE of Carlow, on T16, Co. Carlow. A drawing shows it standing about 10m high. Church said to have been founded by St. Patrick. [73]

Kells; Complete, missing cap. In town of Kells, Co. Meath. 26m high, 4.8m base diam. Site was an ancient royal fort, granted to St. Columba c.550. A refuge for monks from Iona after Viking attacks in 804. A new monastic city was then built. Murchadh, King of Tara, killed in the tower, 1076. 3 High Crosses. [47]

Kilbarry; Vanished. On W. shore of Lough Forbes, Co. Roscommon. Destroyed by great storm in 1770s. The capstone is preserved on the cemetary wall and other stones from the tower are lying nearby. [38]

Kilbennan; Ruinous. 4 km NW of Tuam, Co. Galway. 16.5m high, 4.8m base diam. Monastery founded by St. Benen in 5th C., a disciple of St. Patrick. Monastery burnt in 1114. [24]

Kilcoona; Regular ashlar stump, with joggle-jointed stones. Off the N84, 6 km SE of Headford, Co. Galway. 3.0m high, 5.0m diam. Founded by St. Cuanna, died 650, who collected many learned men around him at this church. The last tower known to be erected, 1238. [25]

Kilcullen; Bottom half of tower. 2 km S. of Kilcullen village, Co. Kildare. Monastery founded by St. Iserninus, companion of St. Patrick, died 469. Monastery plundered by Danes 936 and 944, and burnt 1114. Tower damaged during a battle of 1798 rebellion. [66]

Kildare; Complete tower, battlements replacing conical cap in 1730's. Beside Kildare cathedral. 32.6m high, 5.4m base diam. Nunnery founded by St. Brigid, died 525. Finely decorated doorway. Tower traditionally inhabited by a falcon since St. Brigid's time. Fitted with ladders and floors enabling visitors to climb up inside. [64]

Kilkenny; Complete tower, missing cap. Beside Kilkenny cathedral. 30.2m high, 4.5m base diam. Founded by St. Canice in 6th C., burnt in 1085 and 1114. Fitted with ladders and floors, can be climbed. [76]

Killala; Complete tower with cap. 12 km NW of Ballyina, Co. Mayo, on R314. 25.6m high, 5.0m base diam. Monastery reputedly founded by St. Patrick in 5th C. St. Muiredach was first Bishop. Stands beside the Church or Ireland Cathedral under which is an elaborate early Christian souterrain. [19]

Killashee; Half tower on square base. 6 km S. of Naas, Co. Kildare. c10m high. Church founded by St. Auxilius, a pre-Patrician saint, c.400. [60]

Killeany; Stump. At Inishmore, Aran Islands, Co. Galway. 3.0m high, 4.8m diam. Founded c.490 by one of the leading schools in early Christian Ireland. Burnt 1020 and raided by Vikings 1081. Collapsed c.1760. [28]

Killeevy; Ruined base. 8 km SW of Newry, Co. Armagh, on B113. 10.8m high, 4.6m base diam. A round tower on a square base, the tower fell c. 1776. Nunnery founded here in 6th C. by St. Monenna. [15]

Killeshin; Vanished. 5 km W. of Carlow, Co. Laois. Demolished c.1703 by the landlord, thinking it a danger to his cattle. Height measured on ground as 32m. The monastery was founded in 5th C. A ruined church with remains of beautiful 12th C. doorway. [72]

Killinaboy; Featureless stump. Village on R476, 4 km NW of Corrofin, Co. Clare. 3.6m high, 5.1m base diam. Damaged by gunfire in Cromwellian wars. [33]

Kilmacduagh; Complete, with cap. 8 km SW of Gort, Co. Galway, on the R460. 34.9m high, 5.7m base diam. Monastery founded 7th C. by St. Colman Macduagh.

Skeleton found under the tower in 1878 (pg 20). [34]

Kilmacnessan; Stump. Church on Ireland's Eye, an island off Howth promontory, Co. Dublin. 0.5m high, 3.6m base diam. As on Trinity church at Glendalough, a small tower rose from the arched chancel roof. [56].

Kilmallock; Complete tower, lacking cap, incorporated into a medieval church, with battlements added. In Kilmallock town, Co. Limerick. 16.9m high, 5.2m base diam. Monastery founded in 7th C. by St. Mo-cheallog. The ruined church is 13th-15th C. [86]

Kilree; Complete to top windows. 3 km S. of Kells, Co. Kilkenny on R697. 26.8m high, 4.9m base diam. An early church stands 11m to the S. and a High Cross. [79]

Kinneigh; Complete, without conical cap. On the R588, 5 km NW of Enniskean village, Co. Cork. 21.1m high, 6m base diam. Uniquely it rises from a hexagonal plinth and the masonry is of exceptional quality. The 6th C. monastery founded by St. Mo-Cholmog. The tower is described as nearing completion in c.1015. [92]

Liathmore; Foundation only. 6 km S. of Urlingford, Co. Tipperary, on N8. 5.5m base diam. Monastery founded by St. Mochoemog, died 655, aged 413. Site probablyy abandoned about 1050. Ruins of two small churches. [81]

Limerick; Vanished. Stood beside St. Patrick's church in the SE Liberties of Limerick. Its stones were used by the Williamite army in 1690 to construct batteries during the seige of the town. [82]

Louth; Vanished. Co. Louth. In 987 the annals of Clonmacnoise say that the tower of Louth fell in a great wind. Monastery said to have been founded by St. Mochta, a pre-Patrician British saint. [43]

Lusk; Complete, but missing cap. On the R127, 20 km NE of Dublin. 26.6m high, 5.1m base diam. Monastery was founded in 5th C. by St. Macculind. Pillaged 835, burnt 854, burnt 1089 by Munster men with 180 people inside. Tower attached to medieval church belfry. [51]

Maghera; Ruinous. 5 km S. of Dundrum, on B180, Co. Down. 5.4m high, 4.9m base diam. Monastery founded by St. Donard in 6th C. Before 1744 the tower collapsed in a storm and "lay at length and entire on the ground like a huge gun". [13]

Meelick; Almost complete tower, lacking top windows and cap. 5 km W of Swinford, Co. Mayo, on N5. 21.m high, 5.4m base diam. Nothing is known about the history of Meelick apart from an early tombstone affixed to base of tower. Exceptionally well built. [21]

Monasterboice; Nearly complete tower, missing cap. 8 km N. of Drogheda, Co. Louth, on N1. 28.5m high, 5.0m base diam. Monastery founded by St. Buite mac Bronaigh, died 521. In 1097 the tower was burnt with its books and treasures. Two of the finest High Crosses in the graveyard also ruins of two churches. [46]

Nendrum; Stump. 10 km SE of Comber, Co. Down, on the

A22. 4.4m high, 4.2m base diam. Monastery founded by St. Mochaoi, died c.490. Last abbot was "burnt in his own house" in 974 during a Viking attack. [10]

Oran; Stump. 12 km NW of Roscommon town, Co. Roscommon on N60. 3.9m high, 6.0m base diam. Church said to be founded by St. Patrick and the site is close to the royal centre of Cruchain. No ancient references to the site but the nearby Holy Well of Uaran Gared is still venerated. [37]

Oughterard; Delapidated. 5 km NE of Naas, Co. Kildare. 9.5m high, 4.6m base diam. Nunnery founded by a lesser known St. Brigid in 6th C., and burnt in 1096. [61]

Ram's Island; Capless tower of rubble masonry. In Sandy Bay, on E, side of lough Neagh, Co. Antrim. 12.8m high, 4.2m base diam. No history known. [9]

Raphoe; Vanished. Co. Donegal. Tower demolished in 1637 by Bishop John Leslie of Raphoe to build his new house. Monastery founded by St. Columba in 6th C. [2]

Rathmichael; Stump. Village 3 km SW of Cabinteely, Co.. Dublin. 1.9m high, 5.0m base diam. Monastery founded by St. Macthail, died 548. Number of early grave slabs in churchyard. [65]

Rath Blamaic; Demolished 1838, materials used to build the cemetary wall. 2 km NNW of Dysert O'Dea, Co. Clare. Monastery founded by St. Blamaic in 540. [29]

Rattoo; Complete with original cap. On the R551, 3 km SW of Ballyduff village, Co. Kerry. 27.2m high, 4.6m base diam. Monastery founded by Bishop Lughach in the early 6th C. There are two ruined churches nearby and a Sheila-na-gig on the bell-floor. [96]

Roscam; Half tower standing. 10 km E. of Galway, on N6. 11.0m high, 4.8m diam. Monastery founded by St. Odran in 540. Site devastated by Norsemen in 807. [27]

Roscommon; Vanished. In 1050 the men of Breifne burnt the monastery here and its round tower. [36]

Roscrea; Nearly complete, lacking cap and top windows. In centre of Roscrea town, Co. Tipperary. 20m high, 4.7m base diam. Monastery founded by St. Cronan, died early 7th C. Four instances of fire and pillage between 800 and 1174. Tower split by lightning 1131. Top storey demolished in 1798 after use by a sniper. [70]

Rosscarbery; Vanished. Collapsed in a storm in 1285. Site now of Church of Ireland cathedral. Co. Cork. [93]

St. Michael le Pole; Vanished. Demolished in 1778 after serious storm damage. Used to stand in old churchyard just SW of Dublin Castle. Monastery founded by St. MacThail, died 548. [57]

St. Mullins; Stump. 12 km N. of New Ross, Co. Carlow, on R729. 1m high, 5.1m base diam. Monastery founded by St. Moling, Bishop of Ferns & Glendalough, died 696. [78]

Scattery; Complete, damaged cap. On Scattery Island, 2.5 km off Co. Claire coast, Shannon estuary. 26m high, 5.1m base diam. Monastery founded by St. Senan, died 544,

attacked by Vikings 816 and 835. Surrounded by several church ruins and a 15th C. church of the dead. [97]

Seir Kieran; Stump. 8 km SE of Birr, Co. Offaly, on R421. 2.9m high, 5.1m base diam. Monastery founded by St. Kieran of Seir, or 'the old Kieran', possibly a predecessor of St. Patrick. Stands in the graveyard of a 19th C. church, built on the site of the original. [63]

Slane; Vanished. Co. Meath. Monastery founded by St. Earc, died 512. In 945 the tower was burnt by the Danes when full of people and also "a crozier and the best of bells". [48]

Swords; Complete, with cap. 12 km N. of Dublin on N1. 26m high, 5m base diam. Founded by St Columba in 512, attacked 11 times between 993 and 1166. [55]

Taghadoe; Top part missing. 8 km SW of Maynooth, Co. Kildare, on R407. 19.8m high, 5.0m base diam. Monastery founded by St. Tua, about whom little is known. Tower used as coal store in 19th C. for Protestant church. [58]

Tamlaght; Low stump. On A2, 4 km SW of Ballykelly, Co. Londonderry. 1.5m high, base 3.5m square. A conventional round tower rose from this square base. Monastery founded by Finlangan, died 585. [4]

Timahoe; Complete, with cap. 12 km S. of Portlaoise, Co. Laois, on N8. 29.2m high, 5.6m base diam. Monastery founded by St. Mochua, died 657. Finely carved 12th C. Romanesque doorway. [69]

Tomregon; Vanished. 5 km SW of Ballyconnell, Co. Cavan. Monastery founded by St. Brecin, in 7th C. [40]

Tory Island; Ruinous, but complete in height on one side. Co. Donegal. 12.8m high, 4.8m base diam. Founded by St. Columba in 6th C. [1]

Trim; Vanished. Co. Meath. In 1127 Conor MacFearghall O'Loughlin burnt the monastery and the tower, both "full of people". Presumed to be on the site of the Church of Ireland cathedral. [52]

Tuamgrainey; Vanished. Co. Claire. In 964 Cormac Ua Killin died, the Bishop who built this round tower **Drumclift**; Ruined stump. On N85, 4 km NW of Ennis, Co. Clare. 11m high, 4.9m base diam. Monastery founded by St. Conald. [32]

Tullaghard; Vanished. Co. Meath. In 1171 the tower was burnt by Tienan O'Rourke "with it full of people". The tower was still standing 1757. [53]

Tullaherin; Almost complete, and missing cap. E. of Dungarvan, Co. Kilkenny, on N9. 22.5m high, 4.9m beside diam. Monastery founded by St. Kieran in 6th C. Beside it is a ruined mediaval church, partly 10th C., and an Ogham stone, in the wall. In 1121 a falling stone from the tower killed a student in the church. [77]

Turlough; A complete squat tower with cap. 8 km NE of Castlebar, Co. Mayo, on N5. 22.9m high, 5.6m base diam. Nothing is known about this site before a drawing of 1792. Ruinous 18th C. church stands beside. [20]